Platforms for success

A guide for managers implementing

'orm strategy

. Nance

m Alastair Clark,

Lawton,

s, Sal McKeown

and Susan Kozicki

niace

promoting adult learning

>lsc

Leading learning and skills

Published by the National Institute of Adult Continuing Education (England and Wales)

21 De Montfort Street

Leicester

LE1 7GE

England

Company Registration Number: 2603322

Charity Registration Number: 1002775

First published 2007

© NIACE 2007

NIACE has a broad remit to promote lifelong learning opportunities for adults. NIACE works to develop increased participation in education and training, particularly for those who do not have easy access because of barriers of class, gender, age, race, language and culture, learning difficulties and disabiities, or insufficient financial resources.

For a full catalogue of NIACE s publications, please visit www.niace.org.uk/publications

Cataloguing in Publications data

A CIP record for this title is available from the British Library.

ISBN 978 1 86201 325 4

Designed and typeset by Boldface Typesetters, London

Printed by and bound in Grea: Britain by Latimer Trend

Contents

Acknowledgements

We would like to thank the many people whose thoughts have contributed to this publication, including: Sally Betts, Phil Butler, Ali Close, Terry Loane, Ken Lowles, John Moulson, Joan O'Hagan, Tracy Slawson, Martin Thomson, as well as all JISC Regional Support Centre ACL advisors, and the report writers for all LSC-funded learning platform projects.

Introduction

With improvements in Internet access and a real growth in the e-learning skills of adult learners and their tutors, there is a growing expectation that learning opportunities should include access to an online learning platform.

A learning platform is an online space where teachers can present and manage learning activities. These activities can draw on information sources and draw on a selection of e-learning tools such as forums, online quizzes, wikis and online assignments. The term Virtual Learning Environment (VLE) is also sometimes used to describe these spaces and where they are linked to a Management Information System (MIS) they can be known as Managed Learning Environments (MLEs).

This publication aims to help you plan and implement a learning platform. It draws on the experiences and insights of providers who have started this process. Probably the most important message from pioneers in this work is that the process of implementation requires a clear strategic view and a recognition that the full implementation will take several years to complete.

The intention here is not to provide a 'blueprint for action', but rather to suggest some areas for consideration. At the end of most sections you will find activities which can be used with your colleagues to help in developing your plans.

This publication will take you from initial vision and piloting of your platform to the point where you make the resource available to your whole organisation. It will also address some key issues, including managing staff development, providing equality of access and ensuring that copyright is protected.

Developing a platform requires a bold strategic vision combined with practical support and proper resourcing. Where a provider organisation has created this framework, tutors and learners have shown that they can use it to explore some of the very exciting new ways to learn.

Section 1

Getting started

Why do it?

Most of the learning platforms successfully implemented in adult learning have initially focused on meeting an identified need. This has usually been one or more of the following:

- **the provision of high-quality learning materials** (for some/all/specific courses), with the aim of increasing retention and attainment and widening participation. Appropriately deployed, materials on a learning platform enable learners to practise, revise or re-do elements of a course at a time and place convenient to them.

  Related areas include differentiation of learning materials, improving the consistency of the offer to learners and providing progression advice which can be achieved using external materials or tutor-generated materials.

- **the provision of a networking and communications function** A range of internal resources – such as administration documents and materials for tutors, health and safety materials, and information from or for management – can be made available via a learning platform. A learning platform can facilitate communication across the organisation. Further, a learning platform enables tutors to swap ideas and develop a bank of course materials to help with the development of courses.

- **a contribution to change in the organisation** A learning platform has the potential to deliver e-portfolios and staff training. It might also make a significant contribution to the development and implementation of the organisation ICT/ILT strategy and be a driver for more far-reaching changes of culture.

It is usually helpful to consider how far the technology will help you do your present work better and how far it will enable you to change the way you do things. This discussion is usually characterised as a choice between 'sustaining technologies' and 'disruptive technologies'. In this sense, disruptive is seen as potentially very beneficial if it leads to new and better approaches. (See *The Innovator's Dilemma*, Clayton M Christensen, 1997, Harvard Business School Press.)

Who might use a learning platform?

A range of people will use a learning platform for different purposes and will have varying support and training needs. User groups might include:

- learners who want to access learning materials independently of a class

- tutors who – as volunteers, learners, users and as content generators – want easy access to good-quality teaching materials and staff development materials, the ability to share ideas and resources (including lesson plan templates; FAQs; guides on, for example, supporting learners with a disability; hints and tips), and a means of countering feelings of isolation

- managers, who may see a learning platform as a means of supporting tutors and sharing information across curriculum areas

- senior management, who may want quick access to feedback from learners, and who may want to use a learning platform to market the benefits of adult learning or as a means of communication – disseminating information and consulting staff

- support staff, who may be able to use a learning platform to streamline administrative processes, such as collecting learner data

- technical support staff, who may be involved in developing or supporting a learning platform.

Choosing a learning platform

The answer to the previous question will describe what a learning platform needs to do and how it needs to do it.

Broadly speaking, there are two different approaches to learning platform software. The first is the use of open source software, for example Moodle. Some open source platforms have no licence costs, but still have hosting and support costs Alternatively, off-the-shelf products, sold by software manufacturers, have been tried and tested during implementation and beyond. Expertise may therefore be available, though often at considerable cost.

Ferl (http://ferl.becta.org.uk) has a list of learning platform system suppliers. Becta (http:// www.becta.org.uk/) has a useful list of learning platform services framework suppliers; although the learning platforms are aimed at schools, some are already in use in adult learning. Your Joint Information Systems Committee (JISC) Regional Support Centre (http://www.jisc.ac.uk/rsc) can also provide excellent support and advice on this issue.

In addition, you must decide where to host (in other words, store) your learning platform. Once again, there are two main options:

■ **hosting in-house with your ICT department or organisation** This has the advantage of being generally the cheaper option; also, the staff responsible are likely to understand adult learning. It is often worth checking what learning platforms expertise your ICT department has before you take this option.

■ **using the hosting service of a learning platforms system supplier or third party** (for example there is a number of specialist Moodle hosting services). This can free staff to concentrate on developing content or generating use of a learning platform. It can sometimes be a quicker solution, saving time liaising with busy ICT departments as they procure, deliver and install equipment and software. There is a cost associated with adopting this approach – your JISC Regional Support Centre can provide guidance.

A number of other key costs also need to be met:

☐ staff training

☐ licences (Moodle may be free, but there will be hosting, maintenance and administration costs)

☐ user support

☐ project management

☐ ongoing site administration – as the number of users increases, this task escalates

☐ content creation.

Choosing and Using a Learning Platform in Adult and Community Learning (Bob Powell and Geoff Minshull, 2004, NIACE and JISC) has an excellent discussion on choosing a learning platform and, along with conference papers from the 'Beyond the Fringe and into the Mainstream' Ferl online conference (2004), details many of the issues raised here.

Key stakeholders

Decisions relating to the use, type and hosting of a learning platform may depend on who the key stakeholders are. For example, how the learning platform integrates with the local authority website is crucial. Would some of the functions proposed for a learning platform be better run on a local authority extranet or intranet? How does the learning platform relate to the organisation's website? What role is there for the websites of libraries and providers (where appropriate)?

A learning platform offers the potential to develop the work of a provider. You should consider, for example, how the learning platform might extend delivery and how it might help meet funders' key agendas.

Working in partnership

Working with other organisations on a collaborative venture can have many advantages, the principle one being the sharing of resources across the local area.

Organisation and a clear understanding of the roles undertaken by each partner are important to ensure that a good working relationship is maintained. Questions relating to funding, service level agreements, quality standards, intellectual property rights and enrolment processes are just some of the issues to be considered.

Quality issues

There is a potential conflict between encouraging staff to use, experiment with and explore a learning platform and the need to ensure high-quality provision. The approach to quality will set out how much autonomy is allowed by those contributing to the learning platform.

Agreed common templates, layouts, navigation, shared logos and colour schemes can be used to ensure consistency.

However, for learning resources in particular, a variety of strategies can be used to accommodate different preferences in learning style; language appropriate for the target audience may be used; and useful and supportive feedback can be provided, based on learners' responses. Hence a less prescriptive approach may deliver the best results.

Quality processes should cover who is responsible for publishing materials on the learning platform, who checks the quality of the materials, and who checks that the materials work. It might be worth trialling materials or having an evaluation process within, say, curriculum areas. A case can be made for a supportive, constructive approach offering good practice tips and the use of peer groups.

Common approaches are:

■ if materials are for use in only one class or by one group of users – use existing quality systems that are used for handouts.

■ if resources are designed to be shared – make learning outcomes explicit.

> **Ultimately, however, the key factor is the quality of the learners' experience.**

Planning and piloting

It will take several years to implement a learning platform, and good planning is essential for success. The detail of your action plan will need to fit comfortably within the framework of your organisation and align with your strategy for e-learning and the wider goals of your organisation. It is usually advisable to pilot the learning platform before rolling it out across the organisation. A much-used approach is to focus on a small group of curriculum areas initially to run pilot courses. ESOL, ICT, Modern Foreign Languages and Skills for Life are very popular.

A ziggurat diagram (*Chips with Everything*, Edition 10) is a useful model when considering the development stages of your learning platform. The model assumes that staff will use a learning platform before it is used with learners (see page 7).

Ideas to consider

For staff:

☐ provide a 'staff room' containing online staff materials and induction processes

☐ create a resource repository which will enable staff to access teaching materials at different venues

☐ run staff training events – on e-learning and other subjects – using the platform.

For learners:

☐ create pilot courses containing uploaded resources to use within the classroom, and possibly also resources for learners to access from outside the learning environment for additional practice or as part of the learning programme

☐ run taster courses purely online as an example of the 'real' courses.

Further information: Staff Development e-learning Centre (SDELC):
http://www.sdelc.org.uk

How will you know if it is a success?

There is a range of aspects that can help construct a picture of the impact of a learning platform, including:

- **statistics:** usage, registrations, and so on

- **content:** freshness, accessibility, innovative features, quality of data/materials

- **user engagement:** contributions from users, retention and attainment, learner (user) satisfaction

- **skills development:** of staff developing their ICT skills as a by-product of using the learning platform, or developing editing skills as they produce content

- **behaviour:** whether this learning is being applied in contexts other than the learning platform – examples include how staff deploy new ICT skills in other areas of their work, and how new editing techniques are reflected in the production of materials for use in the classroom

- **results:** whether learners attain relevant standards, and staff work more effectively or efficiently.

E-maturity is a key theme of the Department for Education and Skills (DfES) e-Strategy, aimed at measuring the effective use and development of ICT in order to improve teaching and learning. The use of learning platforms can make an important contribution towards the e-maturity of an organisation.

Activity: the learning platform ziggurat

(Adapted from *Chips with Everything*, Edition 10)

This model is intended as a discussion starter and assumes that an important foundation for use with learners is that there should be existing active use by staff of a learning platform for at least some of the following: administration, curriculum support or training. This initial use by staff ensures their familiarity with the system before they start using it with learners.

Above the foundation is the Learning Platform Ziggurat itself. This model suggests that use of the platform should be incremental – 'do not use all the tools at once'. This is one way of considering usage. There is no merit in aiming for a level of usage which is inappropriate or unsustainable. After all, the higher you climb the further you can fall!

1) Circle the foundation staff activities which you have or wish to have on your platform. There are spaces to add other items.
2) Circle the level which you feel is an appropriate level for your use with learners of the platform at present.
3) Resources: List the types of tools, techniques and resources that you would use on your platform.

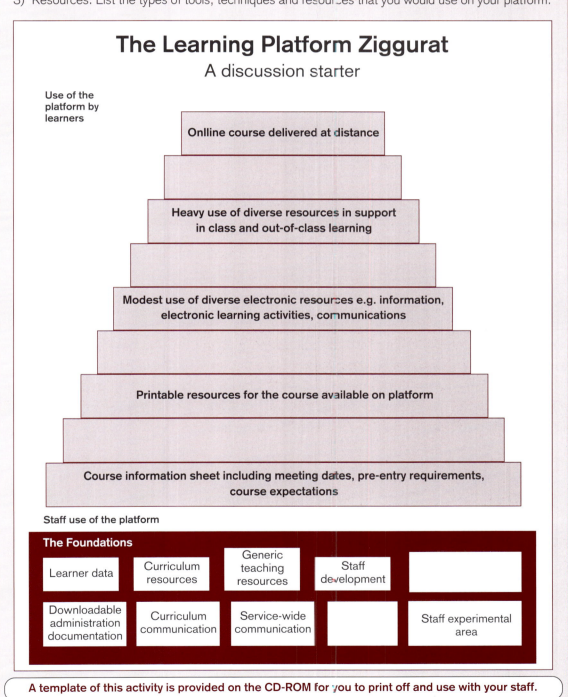

The Learning Platform Ziggurat
A discussion starter

Use of the platform by learners

Onlline course delivered at distance

Heavy use of diverse resources in support in class and out-of-class learning

Modest use of diverse electronic resources e.g. information, electronic learning activities, communications

Printable resources for the course available on platform

Course information sheet including meeting dates, pre-entry requirements, course expectations

Staff use of the platform

The Foundations

| Learner data | Curriculum resources | Generic teaching resources | Staff development | |
| Downloadable administration documentation | Curriculum communication | Service-wide communication | | Staff experimental area |

A template of this activity is provided on the CD-ROM for you to print off and use with your staff.

From piloting to embedding

Long-term strategy

The use and development of a platform requires the commitment of people's time and financial resources over a considerable period. A long-term strategy is needed, describing how the learning platform will be implemented, supported and funded, if the platform is to be cohesive and robust.

The **Getting started** section emphasised the importance of a well-planned pilot. This planning should include forward action planning to ensure sustainability of the platform and implementation across the organisation.

> **Question: Do you have a long-term plan to ensure the sustainability of your platform? How does it fit within the overall strategy of the organisation?**

The initial development of a platform will vary, reflecting the diversity of organisational needs. However, a stage in the development of a learning platform has been identified at which there is a hiatus. A diagram – Moore's chasm – illustrates the gap between the piloting stages of a project and embedding, during which the visionaries and enthusiasts are engaged, but the pragmatists are still to be convinced.

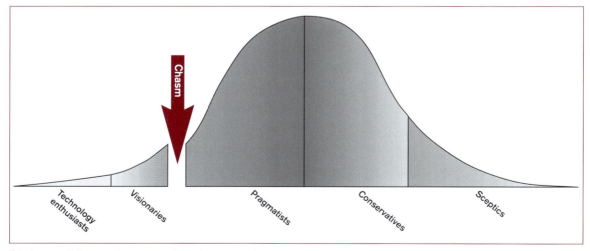

(Adapted from *Crossing the Chasm and Inside the Tornado*, Geoffrey A Moore, 1991, Harper Business)

Anecdotal evidence indicates that the question is not whether a gap will occur, but when.

Staff development can be a major stumbling block, although this is not the only cause of the hiatus. A cohesive strategy should be in place to take the pilot from the initial phase to one where it is embedded within the organisation and has a planned sustainable future. Engaging enthusiasts and visionaries can be relatively easy – this model points to the importance of making a case to pragmatists who in turn can demonstrate a familiarity with good practice which may also influence the conservatives.

Taking stock

When you have piloted the platform, it is useful to take stock of your position. As part of this process, you should evaluate your pilot to learn from the experience before moving to full implementation. This should help you to either develop or clarify your model and assess the robustness of your implementation strategy.

Full implementation will still involve incremental development, as not all staff will be ready and able to adopt the platform, but at this stage you will have finalised your support and management systems. You should also clarify your organisation's approach to such issues as quality assurance and ensuring accessibility.

The following questions should be considered as part of the 'taking stock 'process:

What do I want to use the platform for?

You should be clear about how you intend to use the learning platform – something that varies hugely, depending on the organisational needs and profile. Your ideas may have changed since starting your pilot. Your organisation may not intend to use the platform with learners across the whole curriculum in the medium term, but concentrate on developing a small range of courses and on ensuring that tutors become confident users. With the wide range of adult learning courses and learners, this is a common approach.

The ziggurat model, mentioned in the **Getting started** section (pages 6 and 7), may also help you decide how to use the platform for the development of different courses. Materials for the learning platform can be:

- written by individual tutors for their own use or shared within curriculum areas
- written by small groups of tutors who are paid to develop curriculum content
- written by assigned tutors
- produced professionally.

Question: What do I have? What do I want?

The big picture

How will the learning platform meet the demands of the organisation over the next three to five years? How many learners? Will it be used for both delivery and management of teaching and learning?

The small picture

Content
- is the platform being used as a tutor resource repository?
- is the content going to be accessed by learners within and/or outside the classroom?
- is the content for revision or learning purposes?
- will learners upload content? will they complete online quizzes or tests?
- what quality assurance processes do I have/want?

Management
- will the platform be available for all staff?
- will the platform host some or all of the staff management tools?
- will the platform provide staff training materials? will these be used in a blended approach or autonomously?
- is the management information system (MIS) to be integrated?

Communication
- is the platform for communication between: learners and learners, learners and teachers, tutors and tutors, staff and staff, and so on?
- which communication tools will you use?

It is worth finding out how free, professionally-developed, resources can be used.

Materials can be hosted within a repository, which will allow content packages such as the NLN materials to be reviewed and added to courses. Resources can be accessed from the following websites:

- http://www.aclearn.net/nln-materials
- http://ferl.becta.org.uk – eg Embedding your YouTube video; Keyskills practice tests
- http://www.vts.intute.ac.uk – Virtual training suite
- http://www.qiaresources4adultlearning.net – Online resources

> ## Question: Have you got senior management buy-in?
> Is your learning platform:
> - integrated within the e-learning strategic plan?
> - part of the strategic steering group?
> - included in:
>   - self–assessment?
>   - quality assurance processes?
>   - the reporting system?
>   - communication between senior managers and partners?

Are senior management on board?

For a sustainable and wholly integrated learning platform, the full support of your organisation's leadership is vital. The reports from the LSC-funded pilot and phase one learning platform projects highlight management support as being 'critical to the success of the project'. Without this leadership, the implementation of a learning platform is unlikely to progress beyond the pilot phases.

The publication *Choosing and Using a Learning Platform in Adult and Community Learning* (Bob Powell and Geoff Minshull, 2004, NIACE and JISC) provides some useful examples of the benefits of a learning platform for a organisation – these examples could be used to engage the senior management team.

Having the senior management team represented on the strategy steering group is an important step. The development of the learning platform will have considerable financial implications in both resources and staff time and this will need the agreement of senior management. Linking the learning platform development to a steering group has proved a very effective way of maintaining momentum and ensuring that key stakeholders are represented.

Am I getting staff engaged?

Getting tutors and staff at all levels (curriculum managers, administrative staff, and others) committed to the learning platform is important if they are to take ownership and use the platform effectively. The attitude of staff (other than enthusiasts) can vary from interested to sceptical. Tutors need to see the relevance of the learning platform for both themselves and their learners.

If the platform is difficult to use, whether due to access, navigation or complexity of the system, this presents a barrier to its use by tutors. Consider whether you are making the platform accessible. What technical facilities and support are available to tutors?

You could use the following strategies to provide support for your tutors:

- show example materials and how they could be used within a teaching session
- tap into the creativity of your tutors, identify the level of existing e-learning expertise and how it can be used and upgraded
- provide ongoing support as well as relevant training sessions; for more information, see the **Devising training** section
- provide subject-specific training
- pay staff for attending training sessions
- deliver staff training online.

Harrow – staff resources

Harrow Adult and Community Learning Service developed a staff section of their learning platform and actively encouraged tutors to log in and use it. The resource included the downloadable version of the staff pay claim form and job application forms.

Working for Adult and Community Learning in Harrow 13/09/05
📄 Pay Claim [74kb]
📄 Tutor Application Form [85kb]

What infrastructure do I have? What will I need?

The infrastructure model used during the pilot phase should be analysed to identify any changes needed to ensure it is robust enough to cope with long-term sustainability of the embedded platform. Consider the infrastructure within your organisation and that of other organisations, such as local authorities. Areas to think about include how the learning platform will be accessed. Will it be accessed from classrooms, at home or in a library?

Many providers develop courses within a separate learning platform or on a private part of their main platform. They then transfer them to the live site when confident that the content meets both technical and teaching and learning requirements. Other organisations have separate tutors' and learners' areas.

For some learning platforms, passwords are used to access the main page and then course passwords/keys used to access a specific course. These can be necessary to protect the privacy of a learning group or to comply with copyright. However, passwords can present barriers to use and should be applied with care. Also providing 'guest access' can be a good way to tempt in new learners.

Consider how logins and passwords will be allocated for the number of possible users. Logins and passwords may be set up by course administrators or course tutors.

Many organisations are keen to connect the learning platform and MIS to enable a tie-up between the e-learning platform and learner registration data, and to provide a one-password login to all areas of the organisation's IT system.

Are the hosting arrangements adequate?

The rationale for choosing a particular hosting may have been based on a range of reasons or just on a recommendation. It is worth reviewing your hosting arrangements, to be sure that you have the capacity to 'scale-up' to a larger number of users. Circumstances change and the requirements of your platform will be increasing, so identifying current and future requirements for hosting and support (and the cost implications) are areas to be considered.

Further information

- Ferl: Top tips for embedding a Moodle VLE – http://ferl.becta.org.uk/
- JISC: VLEs and MLEs explained – http://www.jisc.ac.uk
- Aclearn: Piloting to embedding – questions and answers – http://www.aclearn.net

Activity: your plan

Reflect on this section and answer the following questions:

	Staff	Learners	Curriculum areas	Infrastructure/hosting
Where are you now?				
Where do you want to be in: 6 months? 2 years? 5 years?				
How will you get there?				
How much will it cost?				
What is needed from senior management?				
What staff training is needed?				
How will you evaluate the impact of your platform on learners, tutors, staff and the organisation?				

A template of this activity is provided on the CD-ROM for you to expand, print off and use with your staff.

Section 3

Devising training

What are you aiming for?

Many practitioners involved in developing learning platforms have identified that good training and staff support are major ingredients of success.

It is a challenge to devise a training programme that enables your staff to use the learning platform effectively. You should:

- make sure the vision of the purpose of the platform is clear to everyone
- describe the key benefits so that everyone is motivated to learn how to use the platform
- ensure staff can acquire the appropriate level of skills to populate the platform with relevant material for colleagues and learners
- sustain staff training and support beyond initial enthusiasm
- extend staff training and support beyond the enthusiasts (technologists and visionaries) and try to include 'pragmatists'
- consider the training needs of learners and how they will be met
- develop a wide range of flexible learning activities.

Any new initiative needs the active co-operation and support of staff to make it work. A successful innovation requires changes in knowledge, understanding, skills, attitudes and behaviour. So getting the training programme right is a balance of:

effective communication and provision of appropriate skills training across the staff team	recognition of particular curriculum or course issues, and flexibility in supporting and addressing those issues

One project report identified that the key to the success of the learning platform was 'training, training and more training'. You must be prepared to invest in training and support to equip staff to offer the maximum benefit to learners.

Training for staff should address the following areas:

- **the system:** how to access the platform, add and amend content and manage courses
- **the curriculum:** effective practice linking to identified good practice in the relevant curriculum areas and to appropriate materials and online activities
- **pedagogical choices:** enabling staff to identify how best to deploy resources to enhance learning.

Getting staff involved

Although many organisations have a motive for deciding on the introduction of the learning platform, it is likely that most staff will not have been involved in the initial thinking processes.

One motive might be to improve communication among staff by setting up online discussion forums to give information and to answer questions about an event, such as a forthcoming inspection. Alternatively the aim might be to store 'required' documentation, such as proformas for course files or evaluation forms, and explain how they should be used.

Many organisations want to enable learners to find out about courses without visiting a centre – for example, by watching a video of some of the content or listening to comments from other learners.

Understanding the primary objectives of the platform will help staff to see the whole picture.

Are you aiming for:

- better sharing of resources between staff?
- better information and support for learners?
- improved consistency of practice within the organisation?

Incentives and rewards help to motivate people. Can you run a competition to design a quiz for all staff that requires minimal skill levels to complete? A prize for the winner of the quiz itself, but also a prize for the 'best' quiz designer, might stimulate hands-on experience of using one of the learning platform tools. For example, within a team with good ICT skills – the IT support team, or the ICT curriculum team – you could set a challenge to create a quiz for an event or festival. Keep it internal and encourage feedback on the experience in terms of learning how to use the tool.

Practise Moodling

Essex Adult Learning Service has a practice area on their learning platform where tutors can have a chance to practise using the tools. Once tutors feel confident they can then 'go live' with a course for learners.

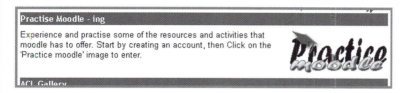

Create an area on the platform for:

■ a staff room – where internal documents are stored, where suggestions can be posted, and where meetings are advertised

■ an informal staff room sometimes called 'the water cooler' (American), 'play room' (family learning and childcare tutors), 'common room' (academics), or café (anyone) where people can 'chat' without constraints

■ play area(s) – these can be either individual areas or joint areas where tutors and staff can experiment with the tools available within the platform.

Work with the professional development programme to try and get the use of the platform discussed in a wider range of training than just ICT. For example, quality improvement sessions or introducing RARPA (recognising and recording progress and achievement).

Designing the training programme

Assessing requirements

The first step in a training programme is often a training needs analysis (TNA). For the use of a learning platform, a TNA is not always useful – the learning platform may be new, and defining needs can be difficult. However, a skills checklist related to the platform features may prove productive. A questionnaire distributed before and after training sessions can help participants appreciate the range of features available. For example, you could ask whether participants can:

■ set up a discussion forum
■ reply to messages and start a new topic
■ upload a sound file
■ download a proforma document

- put an event in a calendar
- track learners' progress.

Demonstration Course in Manchester

Manchester Adult Learning Service have a 'demonstration course' on their learning platform.

This allows tutors to see practical examples of how tools like quizzes, Wikis and journals can be used. It also shows how to link to other resources.

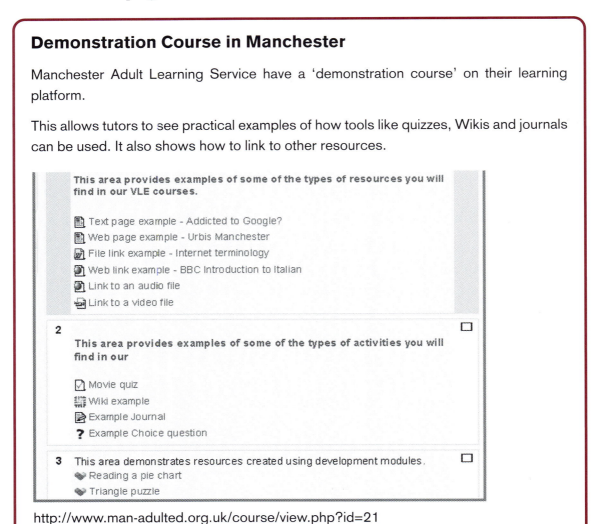

http://www.man-adulted.org.uk/course/view.php?id=21

Improving ICT skill levels

The level of staff ICT skills is a relevant consideration when devising a training programme – if participants are familiar with basic techniques, such as file management and cut-and-paste, they will clearly find it easier to master and apply the same skills in their use of the learning platform.

An ongoing ICT skills training programme which runs alongside all e-learning training is very helpful, especially if it offers staff both an opportunity to acquire an additional qualification, such as ECDL or ITQ and specific job-related training.

Targeting training

Design the training sessions to meet the aims of the whole project. Identify the early key benefits and target initial training at the staff who will gain most from these benefits. You need to consider who to target for training. Options include:

■ **using a curriculum approach** Many organisations have found that organising e-learning training in curriculum groups has been most effective, and this is equally true for learning platform training. Leaders of training understand the needs of their team and – often having only recently acquired the necessary skills and understanding themselves – can provide valuable insights.

To select curriculum groups, consider the size of the team, their likely enthusiasm for adopting the use of the platform, what access to resources (PCs, laptops, Internet) they have, and what interest has been expressed in the platform by the team leaders.

As skills improve, encourage a curriculum 'champion' to set a model for other teams. Some organisations have created 'buddy' or mentor schemes – these can work well across teams as well as within one team.

■ **starting with willing volunteers** Simply advertising a series of training sessions and working with the early adopters can also be effective. One advantage of this approach is that staff in any curriculum area can get involved from the beginning and become skilled and enthusiastic about using the platform. Curriculum areas that might be thought less likely to benefit, such as performing arts or health and fitness, are not excluded.

Supporting a champion and developing buddies and mentor systems is still valuable.

Setting up a support system

As staff begin to upload courses and work independently outside the training sessions, you should ensure adequate and prompt support is available. You might be able to invite members of a technical support team to attend training sessions so they are aware of the issues as they arise.

If support comes from an external source, advising the support team of periods of increased usage by newly-skilled users may help them to respond more efficiently.

Often, the majority of support comes from the manager of the learning platform implementation – perhaps an ICT curriculum manager. In this case, recognition of the time and the administrative support required (for example, for enrolling learners) is essential for a sustainable development.

Online help and support

The platform can offer tutorials or 'how-tos', frequently-asked questions (FAQ) and discussion forums for exchange of information on using the various platform features.

For example, a training session may cover how to upload an image or a video file, but have little time to cover issues such as compression and appropriate file formats – this can be covered by learning materials within the training course.

A successful method of providing how-tos is to use screen capture software and video to create tutorials which demonstrate the steps involved. This is best accompanied by sound and text. Getting staff to create these themselves within a training session can be productive as they may then use the skills to create demonstrations of skills relevant to their subject.

However, many staff want to talk to someone who help them solve their difficulties. It may be possible to offer a telephone support service, a drop-in training session, or a time when a trainer or champion can be available in a staff room or online.

Using the platform with learners

While learning how to create courses on the platform, it is possible to lose sight of pedagogy. Training should offer constant reminders and opportunities to consider the teaching and learning benefits of each feature of the platform and the lesson and course-planning approaches supported through the use of the platform itself.

Take time to consider whether tutors can train learners themselves, or whether they need help.

In Tower Hamlets a member of the council staff was asked to offer a short course in basic Sylheti. Sylheti is primarily a spoken language so the emphasis of the course was on listening and speaking. The face-to-face course was supported by a space on the learning platform where learners could listen to sound files of the basic phrases used in class.

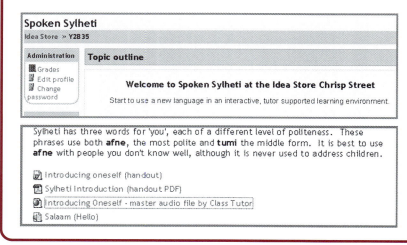

Derby

A tutor in a digital photography class asked students to use an online forum to record and reflect on what they had learned. This provided both a consolidation of the learning and evidence for the learner of his or her progress.

Re: Feedback on the Resolution Session

by Ann Wilby – Tuesday, 21 November 2006, 11:59 AM

I got on very well today,and I really enjoyed this session, because I understood what Elly was saying and the handouts are very understandable. I think The resolution of more pixels the picture can have to the inch has finally got through to me today. More pixels to the inch means better quality, when printed out.

http://www.derbylearn.net/moodle/mod/forum/discuss.php?d=152

Planning next steps

Some staff will quickly adopt the use of the tools on the platform and integrate them into their practice. Involving these staff in the planning of ongoing training and reviewing the platform implementation, and perhaps inviting them to join a steering group or ILT forum, can help ensure that more in-depth training is appropriate. It can also help to promote understanding of any limitations on development and the need to comply with regulations, such as copyright laws (see the **Copyright** section).

Evaluation

The success of the training programme can be measured by the extent to which use of the platform becomes commonplace. As well as taking feedback from staff about the content of the sessions, monitor the activity that takes place after sessions and perhaps set tasks and targets.

Recognising that adoption of a platform is a slow process and setting realistic expectations is important. If you achieve more than you expect, that is better than aiming too high.

Share your experiences with other organisations so that you can 'benchmark' your own situation.

Activity: planning training

Use the questions in this diagram to think through your training plan. Then use your notes to create a SMART action plan – **S**pecific, **M**easurable, **A**chievable, **R**ealistic and **T**ime-bound actions can be regularly reviewed and help to create a sense of achievement.

What do we want the platform to achieve?

Who needs to learn what skills?

Consider the following questions:

Training sessions

How many sessions will there be?

How many participants will there be?

What resources will be used?

What tasks will there be between sessions?

What standards will be applied?

What ongoing support will be provided?

Have access and permission rights been considered?

How will training be evaluated?

How will learners be trained?

A template of this activity is provided on the CD-ROM for you to print off and use with your staff.

Thinking about copyright

What is copyright?

When publishing materials on a learning platform, you must consider copyright. This includes the rights of the person or organisation creating new materials for the platform and the rights of third parties when materials are drawn from other sources.

> "Copyright is the right of the originator of a literary, dramatic, artistic or musical work to control the reproduction and publication or performance of the work." (JISC briefing paper 19)

Copyright protection gives control of the right of copying to the authors/creators or to anyone to whom they have transferred the right.

As materials are much more visible in an electronic environment than in a classroom, it is extremely important that your organisation does not allow copyright material to be used inappropriately.

What material is protected?

Third-party material that you may want to use in your learning platform includes:

- non-digital materials, eg books and reports
- digital images, eg photographs or scanned photographs
- excerpts from films or sound recordings.

It is usually necessary first to obtain express written permission from the rights holder(s) to include digital material in your learning platform. You should only upload copyright materials to your learning platform if:

- you or your organisation own the copyright, or
- you do so under the terms of a licence, or
- you have the explicit written permission of the copyright owner(s).

If the material does not already exist in digital format, you need express written permission both to convert it to a digital format and to include it in the learning platform.

How long does copyright last?

The length of copyright protection depends on the type of copyright work, but generally UK protection rights are:

- **literary, dramatic, artistic and musical works:** lasts for the life of the author plus 70 years from the end of the year in which the author died
- **publications:** lasts 25 years from the end of the year in which the edition was first published
- **sound recordings:** expires 50 years from the end of the year in which the recording was made or, if released within this time, 50 years from the end of the year of release
- **films:** expires 70 years after the end of the year of the death of the last to survive of the principal director, the authors of the screenplay and dialogue, and the composer of any music specially created for the film
- **broadcasts:** expires 50 years from the end of the year in which the broadcast was made or the cable programme was included in a cable programme service
- **databases:** expires 15 years from the end of the year in which the database was made, or 15 years from the publication date if it was published within 15 years of creation.

(Adapted from Staff Development E-Learning Centre (SDELC), *Legal issues with e-learning*: http://www.sdelc.org.uk)

Using images

Unless for an examination or assessed work which contributes to a learner's final mark, express written permission from the rights holder(s) is needed both to digitise, and to include in a learning platform, images of all kinds.

Some image banks provide copyright-free images:

- Scran: http://www.scran.ac.uk
- Images2Teach: http://www.images2teach.net

You should, however, include an acknowledgement if you use an image from one of these sources.

Using sound and video recordings

Before you put commercially-produced recordings, other broadcast material or extracts from them into a learning platform, you must first obtain express written permission.

However, there are some sources of copyright-free audio and video recordings which you can use on your learning platform. Creative Commons (http://creativecommons.org) is a non-profit-making organisation which provides free tools for authors, scientists, artists and educators easily to mark their creative work with the freedoms they want it to carry. You can search the website for Creative-Commons-licensed work.

Using web pages

Web pages and other material on the Internet are protected by copyright. A single web page may contain different copyrights – for example, the text may be protected separately from any artwork, logos or graphics. Unless the web page expressly waives copyright, you may not copy the material for use in a learning platform without the express written permission of the rights holder(s), unless it is for an examination or assessed work which contributes to the student's final mark.

Linking is a more usual way to make use of a web page. Always link to the home page if you can, as this may carry important information which should not be bypassed, such as copyright notices and advertisements. When linking to a web page, consider the following guidelines:

- if you need to link to a page beyond the home page, obtain written permission from the rights holder(s).
- unless you have first obtained written permission to use logos or graphics as links, use text links.
- do not display someone else's web page in a way that may give the impression that it is your work.
- draw learning platform users' attention to any copyright notices on the web page(s) to which you link.

Using tutor-created materials

Tutor-created resources may be used in a learning platform. Before materials are uploaded, however, confirm that the tutor owns the copyright – check that ownership is not with a previous employer and that the resource is not the result of an unauthorised adaptation.

Obtaining permission

When seeking to obtain permission from rights holder(s), decide what material you need to clear and how it will be used. You will need to ask for permission if the materials are to be downloadable and printable as well as just being included in the learning platform. Ask for exactly what you want. Provide details, such as numbers of students and where they are based – for example, will you offer off-site access to the learning platform?

Also consider the following when seeking permission to use copyright material:

- **allow plenty of time to obtain permission:** It may take time to track down the copyright holder, they may be slow to respond or they may refuse to grant permission for use.
- **get permission** in writing, preferably on headed paper rather than by e-mail.
- **tutor contracts should cover legal ownership of created resources:** This is especially important for part-time tutors who may work for more than one organisation. It is also important if your organisation wants to use the resources if the tutor leaves your employment.
- **you can declare copyright on your material:** If you are the author of a resource, you can declare copyright on it by marking it with 'copyright' followed by your name and the year of production.
- **obtain permission for photographs of learners:** When including photographs of learners on your learning platform, make sure each learner signs a permission form which includes a statement on how the image will be used.

Resources on copyright

- JISC (Joint Information Systems Committee): http://www.jisc.ac.uk
  - *Copyright and Intellectual Property Rights* (JISC briefing paper no. 19): This paper provides a brief overview of copyright and intellectual property rights issues for those publishing learning materials through a learning platform.
  - *Copyright and Licensing Guidelines*: Guidelines for good practice in the development of computer-based materials.

Activity: quick copyright quiz

1. All web pages are copyright materials, even if they do not have the copyright symbol displayed. True or False?

2. A tutor wants to upload a presentation that he/she created last year for use in class to the learning platform. Is this acceptable under copyright law? Yes or No?

3. One of your team wants to upload some materials that he/she created in a previous job to your learning platform. Should you:

   A   Go ahead – it's all for the same purpose: education?

   B   Check her contract with her last employer?

   C   Tell her to get permission from her last employer?

4. In a learning platform activity, you include a selection of clip-art and music and a lesson plan detailing how to use the resources. Is this acceptable? Yes or No?

5. Blank forms, ideas, titles and names found online are not considered to be 'original works'. True or False?

There is a range of tools you could use to make this quiz interactive, for example Word, PowerPoint or Survey-Monkey. The use of voting pads would also work well

Answers

1. Answer True. A revision of copyright law in 1989 stated that it was not necessary to include a copyright statement and / or symbol on an original work in order for it to be protected by copyright law.

2. Answer Yes. Provided there were no copyright materials included in the presentation including images and photographs. If the tutor created the presentation while in the employment of another organisation, the copyright of the material may belong to the organisation, so it is worth checking.

3. Answer B and C. The resources produced by staff in the context of their employment will normally belong to their employer. It is advisable to check the contract of employment or ask permission from the previous employer before uploading the material.

4. Answer No. You can use legitimately acquired material in the classroom; however, it cannot be redistributed in another form without express permission.

5. Answer True. These items are not considered to be original works – unless the ideas are expressed in the form of a work, such as in a book.

A template of this activity is provided on the CD-ROM for you to print off and use with your staff.

Thinking about accessibility and usability

What is accessibility?

Accessibility is about making sure that your learning platform can be used by everyone. This means taking account of the needs of users including those who are blind, deaf, dyslexic or have learning difficulties. Your 'anticipatory duty' under the Disability Discrimination Act requires that you have a strategy in place to make your learning opportunities available to all learners.

A plan to develop a learning platform needs to take account of the needs of all learners and staff, including those with disabilities. There are both technical and pedagogical practices which need to be adopted to make a learning platform truly accessible.

If a single resource cannot be made to meet the needs of every learner then the law in the UK requires providers to make 'reasonable adjustment'. It is not sufficient to wait until a user with a particular need makes a request – under the law, your anticipatory duty requires that you have a strategy in place to enable all potential users to access your resources.

Designing for accessibility

In developing your platform, it is important to communicate the importance of designing for inclusive learning. This message should be targeted at technical staff and teaching staff alike.

The demands of accessibility can appear daunting at first. You can obtain help and support from a range of specialist organisations – see 'Sources of advice and support' in this section. With careful planning and good internal communications, it is possible to demystify the question of accessible e-learning and motivate staff to commit themselves to providing it.

To meet learners' needs, good initial assessment is essential. This initial assessment of learners' support needs should be included at the start of a course and fits well alongside the initial learning assessment in the RARPA (Recognising and Recording Progress and Achievement) five-stage process.

Web designers and learning platform developers find that the flexibility and adaptability they incorporate to meet the needs of disabled users also benefits many people who might not consider themselves disabled. Good design for particular needs can lead to better design for all.

What is usability?

Good web usability is about designing online resources in such a way that your users can find what they are looking for quickly and efficiently and then use what they have found easily.

Platforms should always be tested for usability, and this usability should be considered alongside accessibility. Once people have accessed your learning platform, perhaps by using some form of assistive technology, they need to be able to navigate around it with ease.

The language used should be plain and clear to take account of the reading levels of all users. Online tools can be used to provide a SMOG (Standard Measure of Gobbledygook) analysis of a piece of writing.

As learning platforms encourage interaction, it is important to consider how easy it is for the user to become an active participant in the learning process.

Working towards technical accessibility of your learning platform

Current debates include discussions about whether it is feasible to design for 'all' or whether, pragmatically, you should aim to design for 'many' and accept that for some learners you will need to make "reasonable adjustment" and provide materials in another format. It is important to engage your development team and content creators in this discussion.

You need to try and involve disabled students in the design of your learning platform and encourage them to comment on features they find difficult to use or changes that might help them. Set up testing groups and act on the feedback you receive.

Be aware that some disabled people use assistive or access technology, such as screen-reading software, to access your learning platform. Ask such users to test your learning platform. Ideally, watch them doing so and identify the issues they face. Many visually-impaired users use magnification software which enlarges text on the computer screen. Ask such users how easy it is to navigate your learning platform when using magnification software.

Sources of advice and support

Many other organisations seek to address the issue of accessibility for their websites in general and learning platforms in particular. You can join networks of organisations similar to your own and also seek advice from specialist organisations.

The World Wide Web Consortium (W3C) attempts to agree standards for use of the web. As part of this work, W3C has established a Web Accessibility Initiative (WAI) (http://www.w3.org/WAI). This provides a great deal of advice on good practice and has established three levels of web accessibility: WAI Priorities 1–3. You can test your platform against these levels – specialist companies advertise testing services.

There are also some free online tools which offer a free initial assessment of a web address. This can be a useful way of demonstrating the principles of accessible design.

Most platforms offer software-specific documentation which addresses accessibility and can be found easily on the web. There are also a number of online user communities for specific systems, such as WebCT and Moodle. These often address accessibility issues and can be very useful sources of practical information.

The Joint Information Systems Committee (JISC) funds the work of TechDis (http://www.techdis.ac.uk) which provides an educational advisory service in the fields of accessibility and inclusion. TechDis produces a range of publications and runs a series of events.

Other useful resources: *Inclusive Learning and Teaching: ILT for Disabled Learners* leaflet (JISC www.jisc.ac.uk)

Other specialist organisations include:

- blind users: Royal National Institute of the Blind (RNIB) – http://www.rnib.org.uk
- deaf users:
    - Royal National Institute for Deaf People – http://www.rnid.org.uk
    - British Deaf Association – http://www.bda.org.uk
- users with learning difficulties: Mencap – http://www.mencap.org.uk
- users with Cerebral Palsy: Scope – http://www.scope.org.uk
- support for disabled computer users – AbilityNet http://www.abilitynet.org.uk
- JISC Regional Support Centres – http://www.jisc.ac.uk/rsc

Disability equality

Many institutions and providers are now required by the Disability Discrimination Act and other legislation to produce action plans which demonstrate how they are improving their services for disabled learners and disabled staff. The Disability Rights Commission has produced extensive guidance, available via its website (http://www.drc-gb.org).

The most important element of the scheme is the continual involvement of disabled people in offering feedback and suggesting improvements to services, including access to education provision.

By making improvements to your learning platform, you will be contributing positively to addressing disability equality.

Find out on the Disability Rights Commission website (http://www.drc-gb.org) how you can meet your disability equality duty and contribute to your organisation's Disability Equality Scheme (DES). This should contain a three-year action plan to ensure that disabled people are not subjected to discrimination within your organisation.

Activity: accessibility and usability

When thinking about accessibility and learning platforms you will need to be consider both the infrastructure of the platform and content that is uploaded. Consider how the following areas within your organisation should be addressing accessibility and usability of your platform and its contents.

IT department

Question: To what extent is the learning platform infrastructure compliant with the needs of learners with disabilities? Carry out an initial accessibly assessment of your site using one of the available tools e.g. http://webxact.watchfire.com/

- where do you need to get further information from?
- are your IT staff aware of accessibility requirements? What staff training is needed?
- what else could be done to make the site more user friendly?
- identify where your staff can find out information about software, hardware or adjustments that could be used to enhance the learning experience. Who else needs to know?

Teaching staff

Question: To what extent are your staff considering the accessibility needs of their learners when developing content?

- how will you find out? What staff training needs have you identified?
- how are they user-testing their content?
- where can you get help?
- are staff aware of ways of making 'reasonable adjustment' to materials to meet legal requirements

Learners

Question: Have you involved learners with learning difficulties or disabilities in the design and content of your learning platform? Develop a plan and identify future actions that would be necessary for implementation.

The TechDisc Staff Pack (www.techdis.ac.uk) provides a series of training materials which can be used for staff development.

> **A template of this activity is provided on the CD-ROM for you to print off and use with your staff.**

Section 6

And...what next?

Looking forward

The ways in which learning platforms can be used to transform the learning and teaching experience will extend as technology advances and people become more confident about using the platforms.

Some of the questions for the future include: the need for personalisation of learning, the requirement for learners to have access to a personal space to support e-portfolios, single logins and the ongoing need for good connectivity to enable out-stations to have access to the platform.

Making connections with the management information system

Several management information systems (MISs) are being used to link with learning platforms to create a managed learning environment (MLE). An MLE should provide savings in time spent in administration, in creating courses, in enrolling learners and by tutors using the MIS database.

The full implications of linking an MIS and a learning platform need to be considered carefully. The Joint Information Systems Committee (JISC http://www.jisc.ac.uk) has published a number of briefing documents which help to explain the process.

JANET Roaming and single-password login

The JANET network provides the Internet connection for institutions and connections between regional broadband consortia. JANET Roaming will provide a username and password login regardless of location. This will enable an authenticated, secure and easy access for visitors to JANET sites.

Shibboleth is the new standards-based, open source middle-ware which provides single sign-on and will run alongside ATHENS until 2003, before taking its place. JISC has several briefing sheets about JANET Roaming and Shibboleth.

E-portfolios

Work on e-portfolios in adult learning is at an early stage.

JISC highlights three main purposes for portfolios.

■ **presentation:** containing materials to use for application purposes, for example CVs
■ **learning:** personal and reflective learning
■ **transition:** supporting learners as they move between education sectors.

These purposes differ widely, as do the implications for organisations.

Some organisations are starting to consider providing online space in which learners can place their work. In Moodle, for example, 'courses' have been set up as e-portfolios for learners to use. When learners are work-based, this is particularly useful – it enables assessors to mark NVQ assessments with ease. Some accrediting organisations will require discrete e-portfolios containing assessment evidence.

The logistical issues associated with providing online space for all learners, and the issue of how data is transferred or made available when learners move on, have yet to be resolved. There is also a need for clarification of the overlap between personal online space for each learner, e-portfolios and assessment. Discussions are ongoing regarding the terminology that is being used, and technical standards to ensure e-portfolio functionality and operability across organisations are still developing.

For further information, see:

■ Becta: http://ferl.becta.org.uk
■ ePortfolios: http://www.eportfolios.ac.uk

Online courses

When developing your strategy for the learning platform, the way in which it will be used with learners will evolve. In its initial stages, the platform will probably be used as part of a blended delivery. However, the development of online courses may be something that is appropriate within your organisation. This is particularly useful if the population in the organisation's area is dispersed or rural. The provision of online courses for tutor professional development is recognised as being particularly effective and could be a useful way of developing your tutors' expertise in delivering online learning.

The hosting of online courses carries its own logistical issues and communication considerations that demand careful planning.

Conclusion

While these ideas may be future considerations, linking these to your initial vision and including future developments during your planning process is important. It will ensure that your platform is flexible enough to adapt to changes or developments within the field. If you consider in advance the requirements that your organisation may want to place on the platform in the future, this encourages the sustainability of the learning environment.

Internet Detective in Kent

The Internet Detective is a free online tutorial provided to learners on the Kent Adult learning service. It can be accessed at any time and encourages independent learning by offering practical advice on evaluating the quality of web sites.

http://www.kaesonline.com/

Section 7

Case studies' Top Tips Review

Six case studies have been written around different organisations using learning platforms. These case studies have been included on the CD-ROM accompanying this publication. The following Top Tips are just some of the tips highlighted by the organisations showcased in the case studies.

Birmingham ALS: provides Moodle for their learners with AQUA MIS to manage the VLE, creating a Managed Learning Environment.

Top Tips

1. Get senior academic managers actively committed, otherwise you could end up with a lag between the production of wonderful resources/facilities and their take-up by tutors.
2. Make it clear to tutors who has responsibility for quality assurance of course material. Distinguish between quality assurance for branding purposes and for pedagogical purposes; otherwise your marketing manager will find him/herself fielding queries about teaching issues!
3. Provide guidelines for tutors on copyright issues.
4. Provide templates for learning materials.

Bournemouth ALS: are using Moodle across its three main sites and some 15 or so community venues. It has been used to deliver their Level 4 teacher training programme online.

Top Tips

1. Record interviews with tutors, as part of the evaluation.
2. Record interviews with those who are not using the VLE too to find out why not. This means you can then target them with the arguments which may help to move them on and change their minds.
3. Think about one-to-one sessions to enhance confidence for slow adopters.
4. Embed the VLE into the teacher training programme so that tutors start as learners and use it in their classes

Bromley: Uses a college intranet to focus on the delivery of content. It also uses an in-house MIS in SQL Server that has allowed the development of a simple system for staff and learner logins based on information already held in the system.

Top Tips
1. Don't start thinking, "I must introduce students to e-learning". Look at what you want to do with students, and see if e-learning will help.
2. Tap into the creativity of tutors: start off with tutors who are keen, and then spread the practice.
3. Develop a good relationship with your IT manager. They're only human; don't go in with guns blazing!
4. Make sure your uploaded resources and materials work before unleashing them on to students.

Cornwall Adult Education Service: is using Moodle to reach the 361 venues across the county where travel and transport can be difficult.

Top Tips
1. Don't make Moodle a separate issue. It is just another tool in the ILT armoury and not something special or separate. Stress this regularly.
2. Where possible, use exemplars made by staff. This encourages others to try and it gives a boost to those whose work is chosen.
3. Make sure the portal is password-protected and that staff know that their work will just be on show to their learners and their team and not to everyone. This makes a real difference and reduces anxiety.
4. Whatever the issue, 'Never say No!' There must be a solution somewhere!

Portsmouth: 'Putting the 'e' into ACL', has brought together four local authorities – the Isle of Wight, Portsmouth, Hampshire and Southampton. They are using Moodle for staff development across the county.

Top Tips
1. Mix staff from different areas to improve networking. This also helps with the cross-fertilisation of ideas.
2. Spend some time getting the composition of the steering group right and think about what you want them to do. It shouldn't just be a talking-shop.
3. Show some ready-made resources to get people enthused about what can be done.
4. Pay tutors for some development time and ask them to create, share and evaluate a resource as soon as possible after the training.

Tees Valley: Middlesbrough, Redcar, Stockton, Hartlepool and Darlington are working in partnership to use Moodle as a way of sharing resources across the Tees Valley.

Top Tips
1. Don't opt for secure, small pilots. Encourage everyone to have a go and be creative!
2. Always have a working copy of your VLE for development work.
3. When you put a course on the VLE always consider how are you going to evaluate the course.
4. Ensure that the courses are coded correctly so you can pull the data off easily.
5. Adapt your existing QA systems to incorporate online learning.

Resources

Publications

Beyond the Fringe and into the Mainstream, Ferl online conference, 2004

Chips with Everything, edition 10, January 2006

Choosing and Using a Learning Platform in Adult and Community Learning, Bob Powell and Geoff Minshull, 2004, NIACE and JISC

Copyright and Intellectual Property Rights (JISC briefing paper no. 19, http://www.jisc.ac.uk)

Copyright and Licensing Guidelines (http://www.jisc.ac.uk)

Crossing the Chasm and Inside the Tornado, Geoffrey A Moore, 1991, Harper Business

Guidelines for Fair Dealing in an Electronic Environment, JISC, 1998 http://www.ukoln.ac.uk

Harnessing Technology, Transforming Learning and Children's Services, DfES, 2005

The Innovator's Dilemma, Clayton M Christensen, 1997, Harvard Business School Press

Web Links

Aclearn: (http://www.aclearn.net)

Becta (http:// www.becta.org.uk/)

British Library and the Copyright Licensing Agency (http://www.bl.uk)

Changes in UK copyright law – a joint note from the British Library and the Copyright Licensing Agency (http://www.bl.uk)

Copyright Licensing Agency (CLA) Limited (http://www.cla.co.uk)

Creative Commons (http://creativecommons.org)

Disability Rights Commission (http://www.drc-gb.org).

ePortfolios: http://www.eportfolios.ac.uk

Ferl (http://ferl.becta.org.uk)

Guidelines for Fair Dealing in an Electronic Environment (http://www.ukoln.ac.uk)

Intellectual Property website (http://www.intellectual-property.gov.uk)

Images2Teach (www.images2teach.net)

JISC Regional Support Centres (http://www.jisc.ac.uk/rsc)

Online resources (http://www.qiaresources4adultlearning.net)

Royal National Institute of the Blind (RNIB) – http://www.rnib.org.uk:

Royal National Institute for Deaf People – http://www.rnid.org.uk

Scran (http://www.scran.ac.uk)

Staff Development E-Learning Centre (SDELC), (http://www.sdelc.org.uk)

Support for disabled computer users – AbilityNet http://www.abilitynet.org.uk

TechDis (http://www.techdis.ac.uk)

Virtual training suite (http://www.vts.intute.ac.uk)

Web Accessibility Initiative (WAI) (http://www.w3.org/WAI)

Appendix

Contributions from the all LSC-funded learning platform projects:

Pilot Phase

Buckinghamshire County Council Adult Learning Service
Cornwall County Council
Kent County Council
Southend-on-Sea Borough Council
WEA East Midlands
WEA North West

Phase 1

Bromley Adult Education College
Derby City Council
Derbyshire Adult Community Education Service
Gateshead Council
Leicestershire County Council
Lincolnshire County Council
London Borough of Tower Hamlets
NE Lincolnshire Council
North Tyneside Council
Poole Borough Council
Sunderland City Council
Surrey County Council
Telford & Wrekin Council
Walsall Metropolitan Borough Council
Wolverhampton City Council

Phase 2

Bolton Council
Bournemouth Adult Learning
Brent Adult and Community Education Services
City of Wakefield Adult and Community Education Service
Community Education Lewisham
Coventry Adult Education Service
East Riding of Yorkshire Council Adult Education Service
Essex Adult Community Learning
Hounslow Adult and Community Learning Service
Knowsley FACE

Manchester Adult Education Service
Medway Adult Learning Service
Northumberland County Council Adult Education Services
Rutland Adult Education
Service Birmingham/Birmingham Adult Education Services
Tees Valley:
    Darlington Adult Education Service
    Hartlepool Adult Education Service
    Middlesbrough Adult Education Service
    Redcar & Cleveland Adult Learning Service
    Stockton Adult Education Service
WEA London
West Sussex Adult Education Service
York Adult & Community Education Services

Phase 3

Blackpool Council Adult and Community Learning
Cheshire County Council
Hertfordshire County Council
Hull Community Learning
Reading Borough Council
Redbridge Institute of Adult Education
Rochdale Metropolitan Borough Council
Slough Borough Council
Southampton City Council Adult and Community Learning
West Berkshire Council Adult and Community Learning
Wiltshire County Council Family Learning Service